MAZE

FOR KIDS

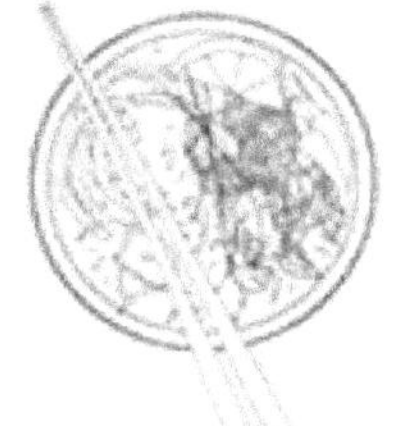

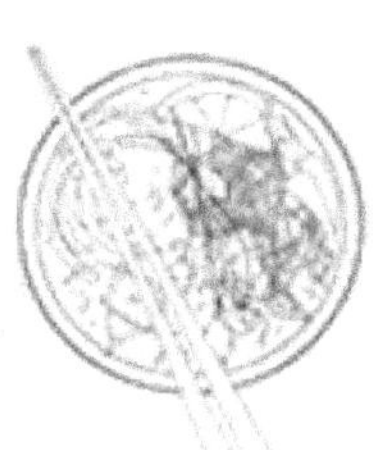

MAZE BOOK

SOCIAL MEDIA

 /MySweetBooks1

 /MySweetBooks1

 /MySweetBooks1

 /MySweetBooks

Email Us : mysweetbooks1@gmail.com

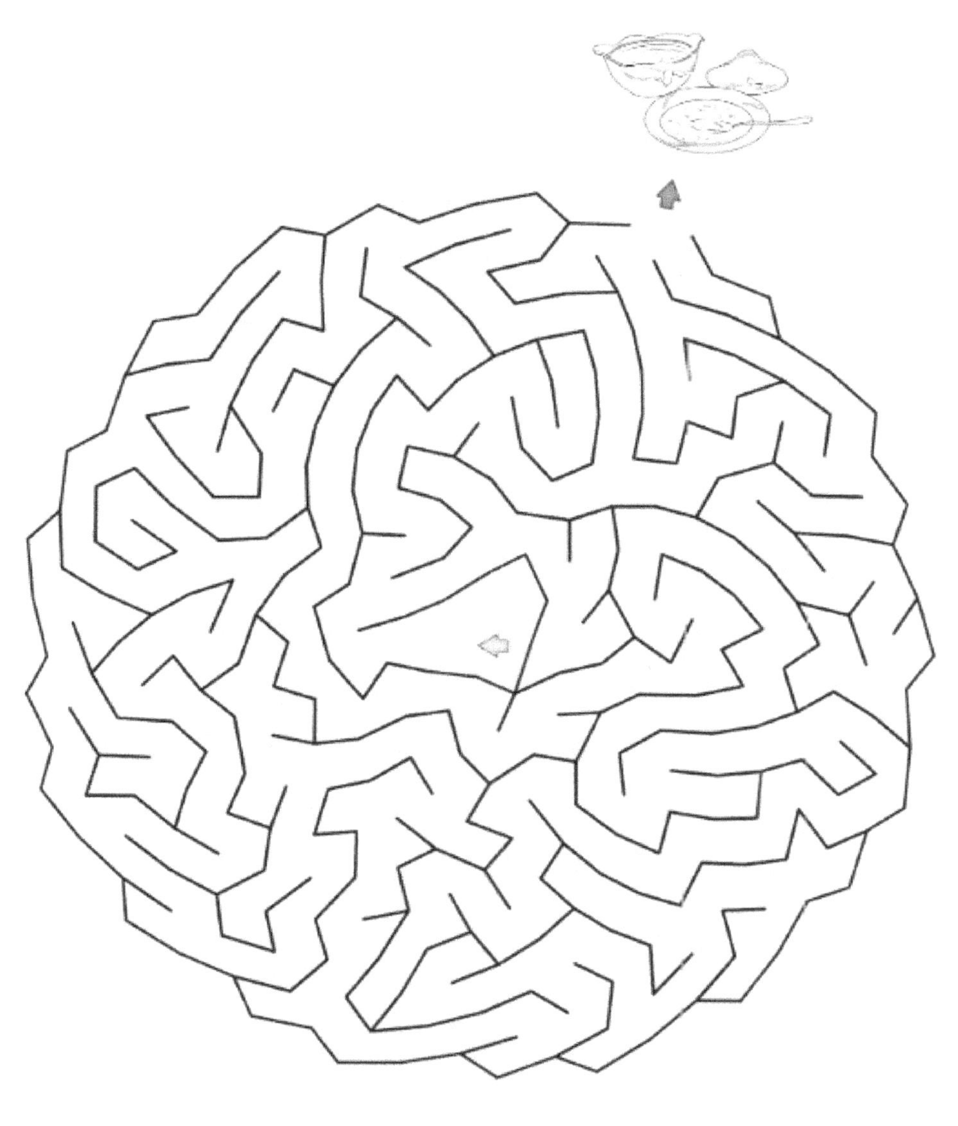

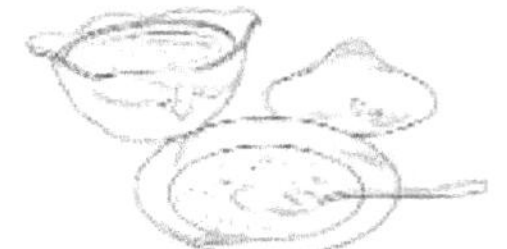

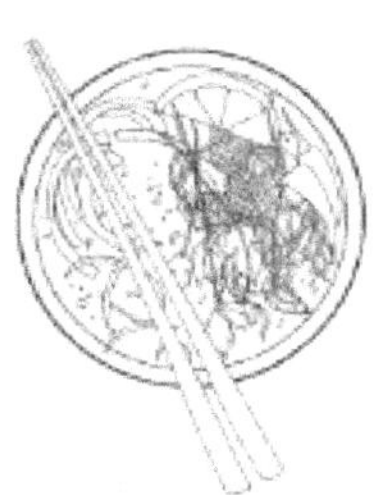

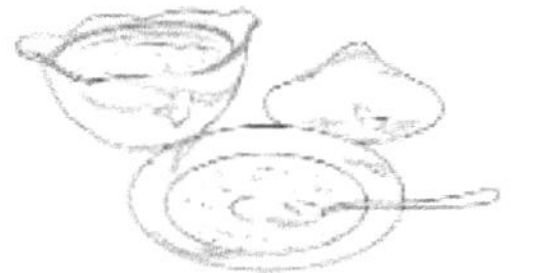

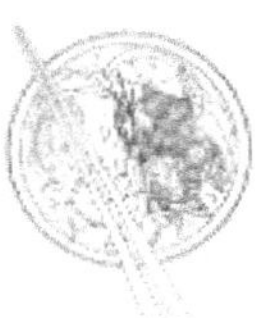

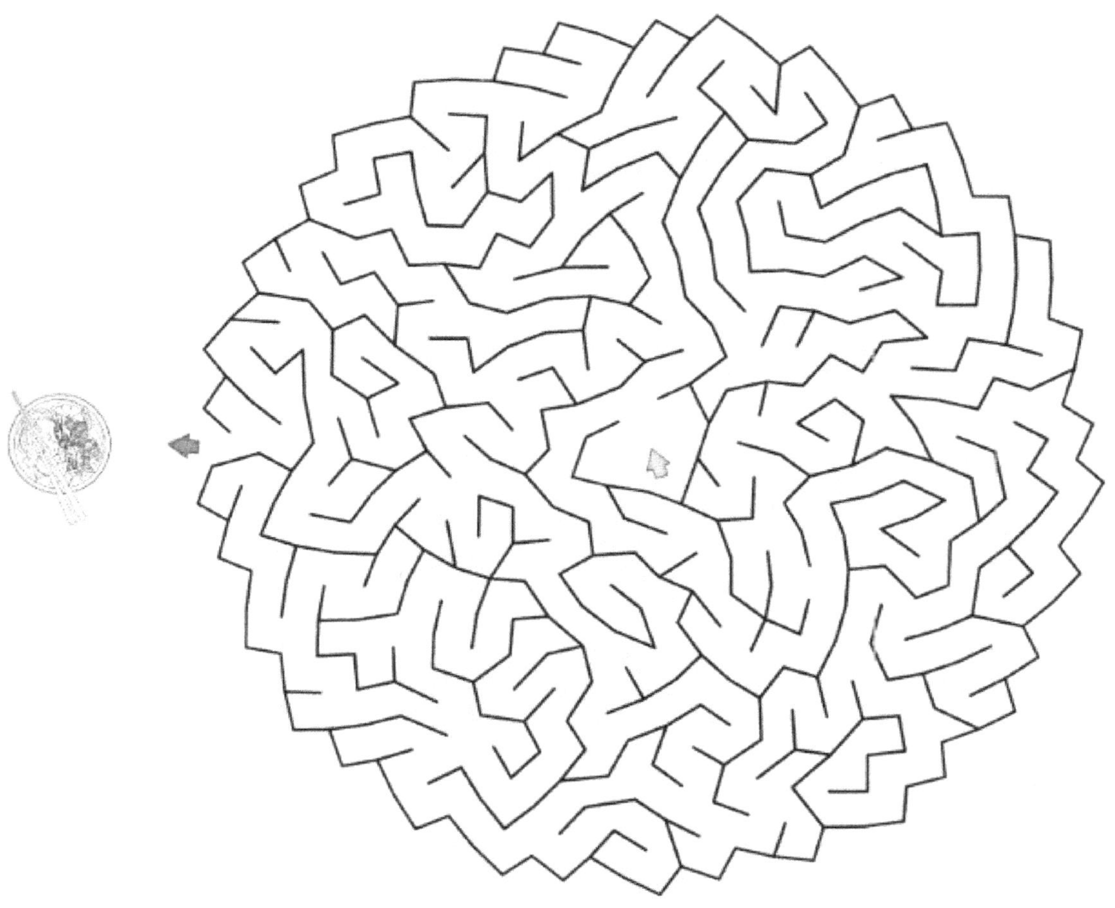

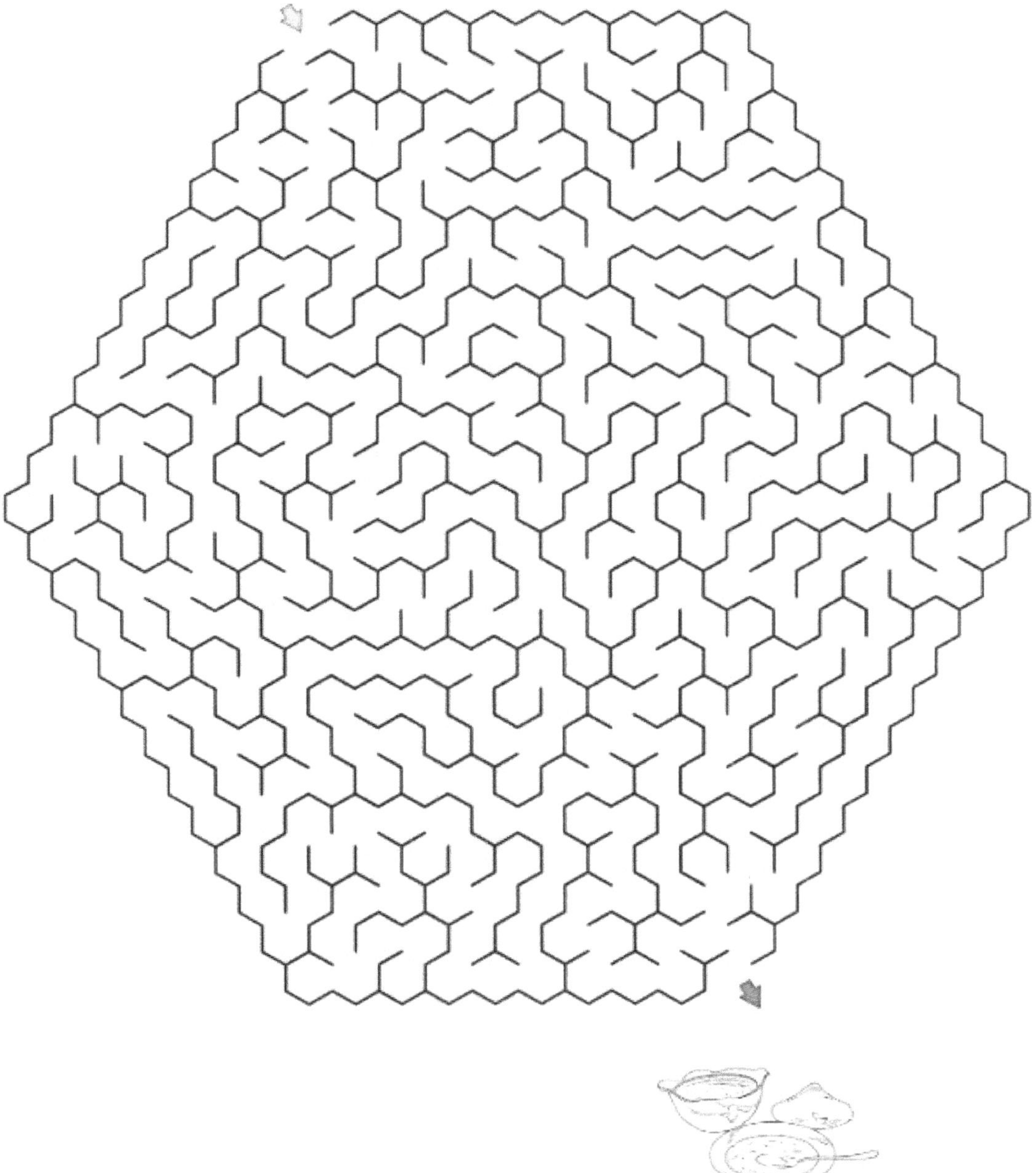

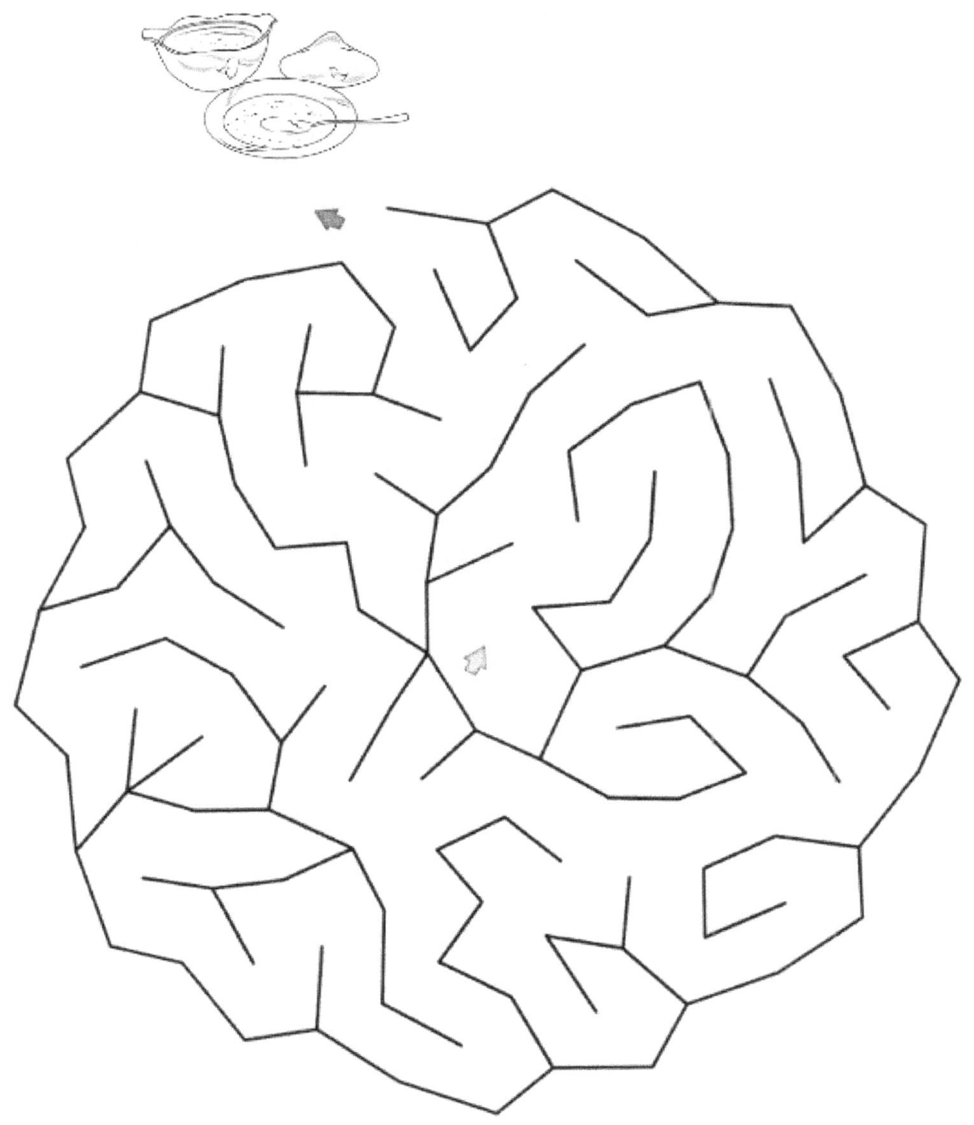

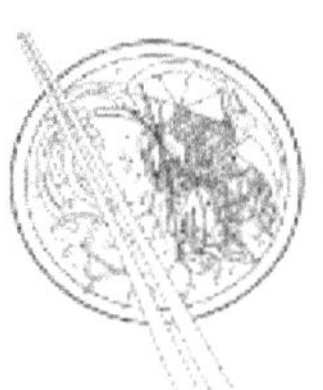

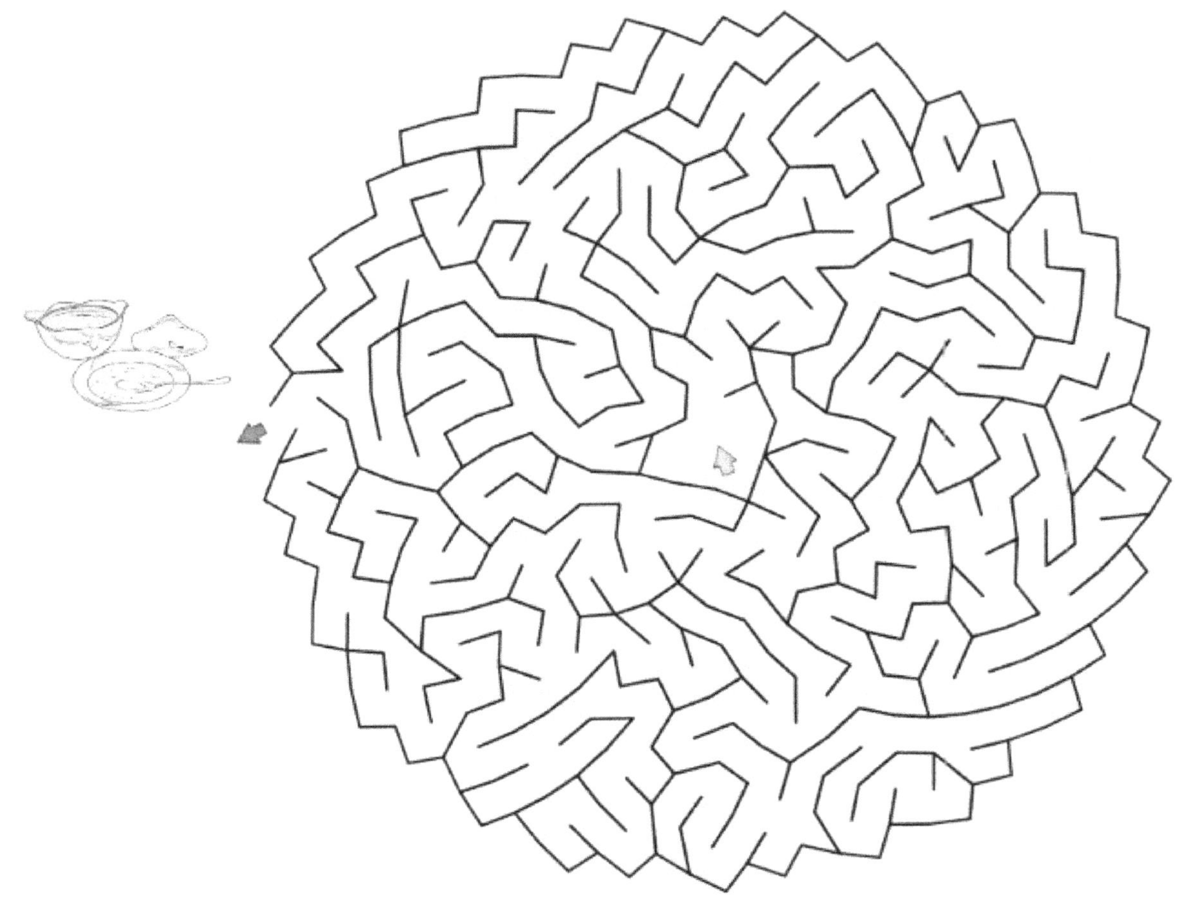

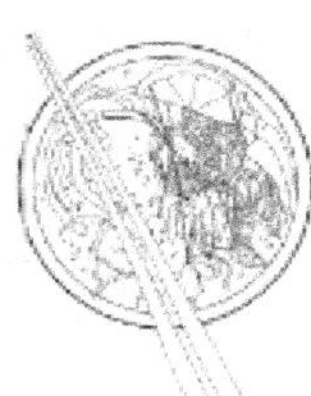

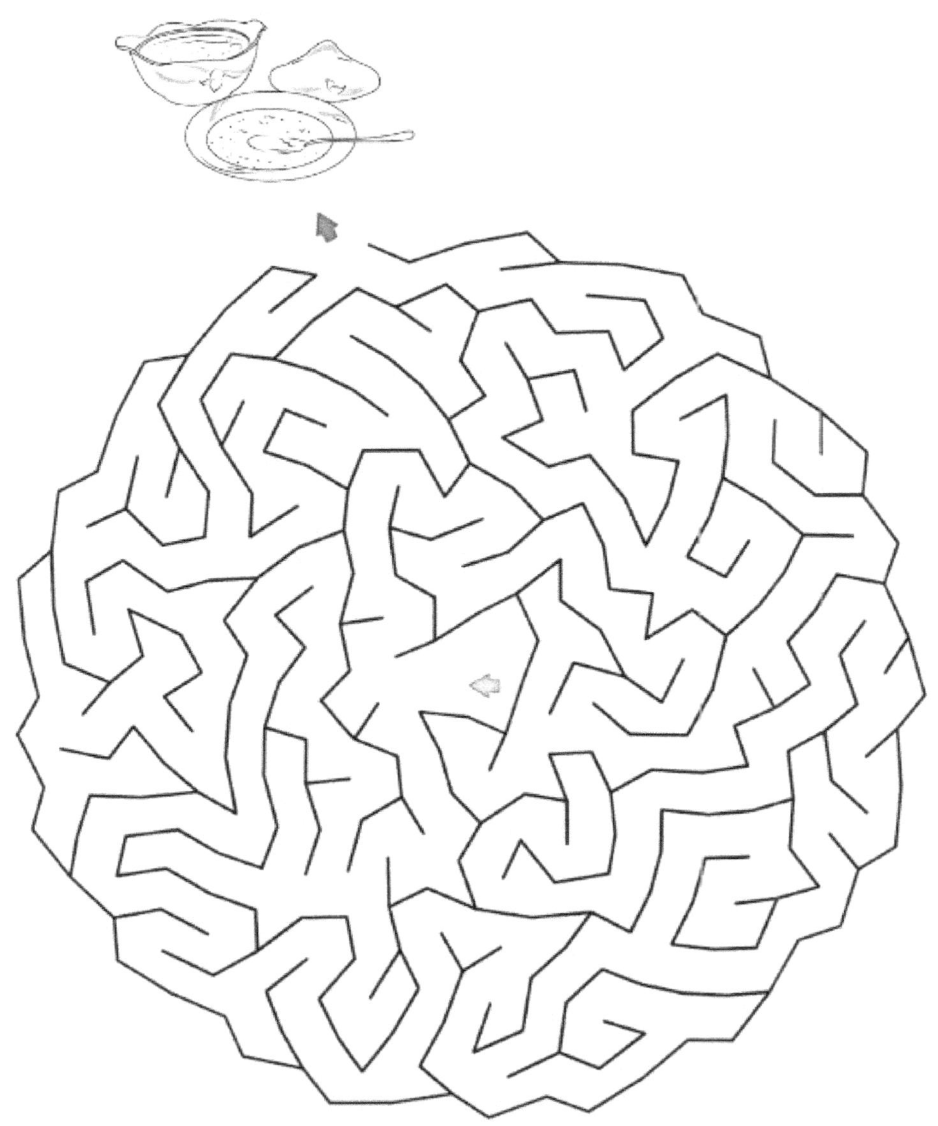

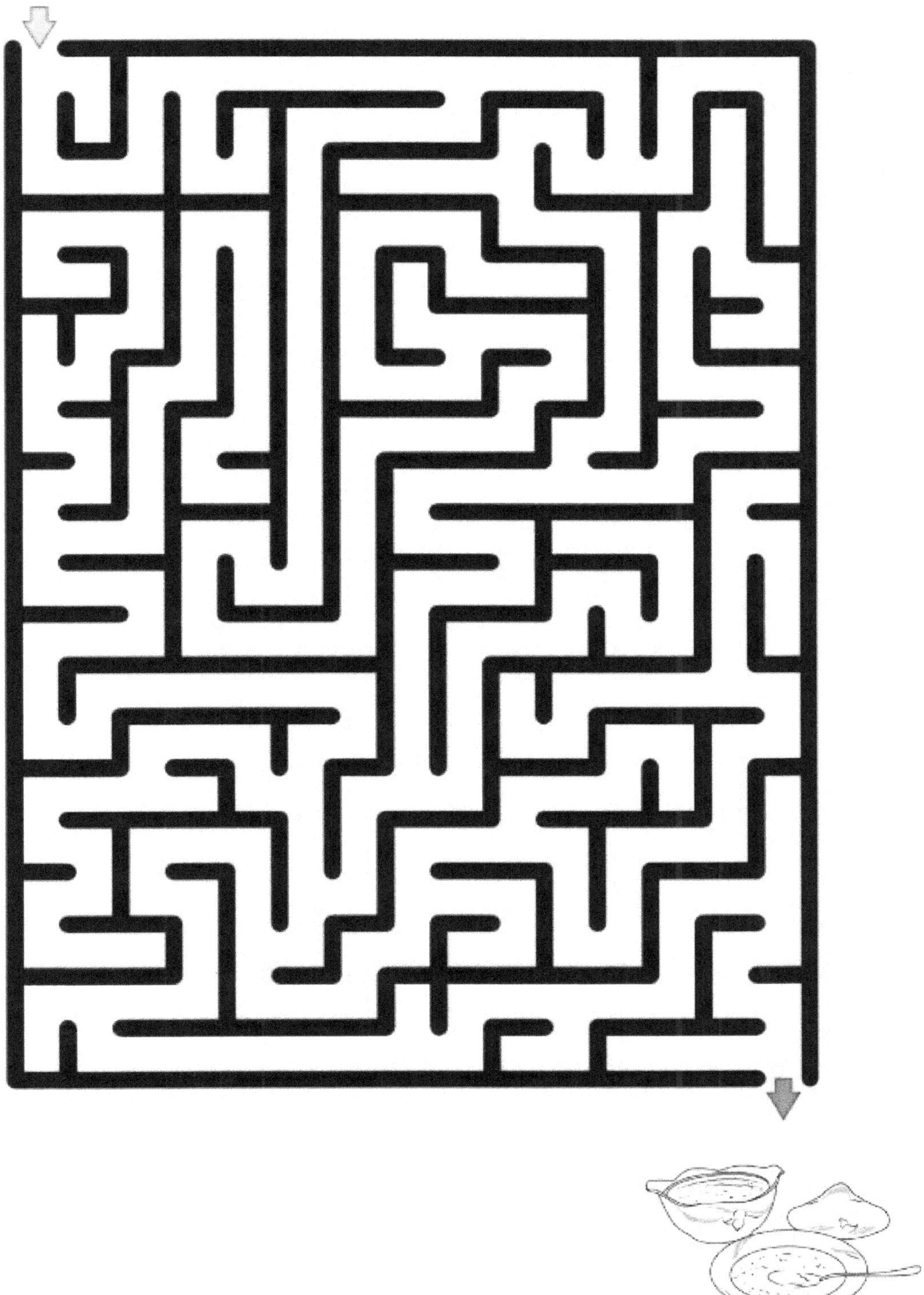

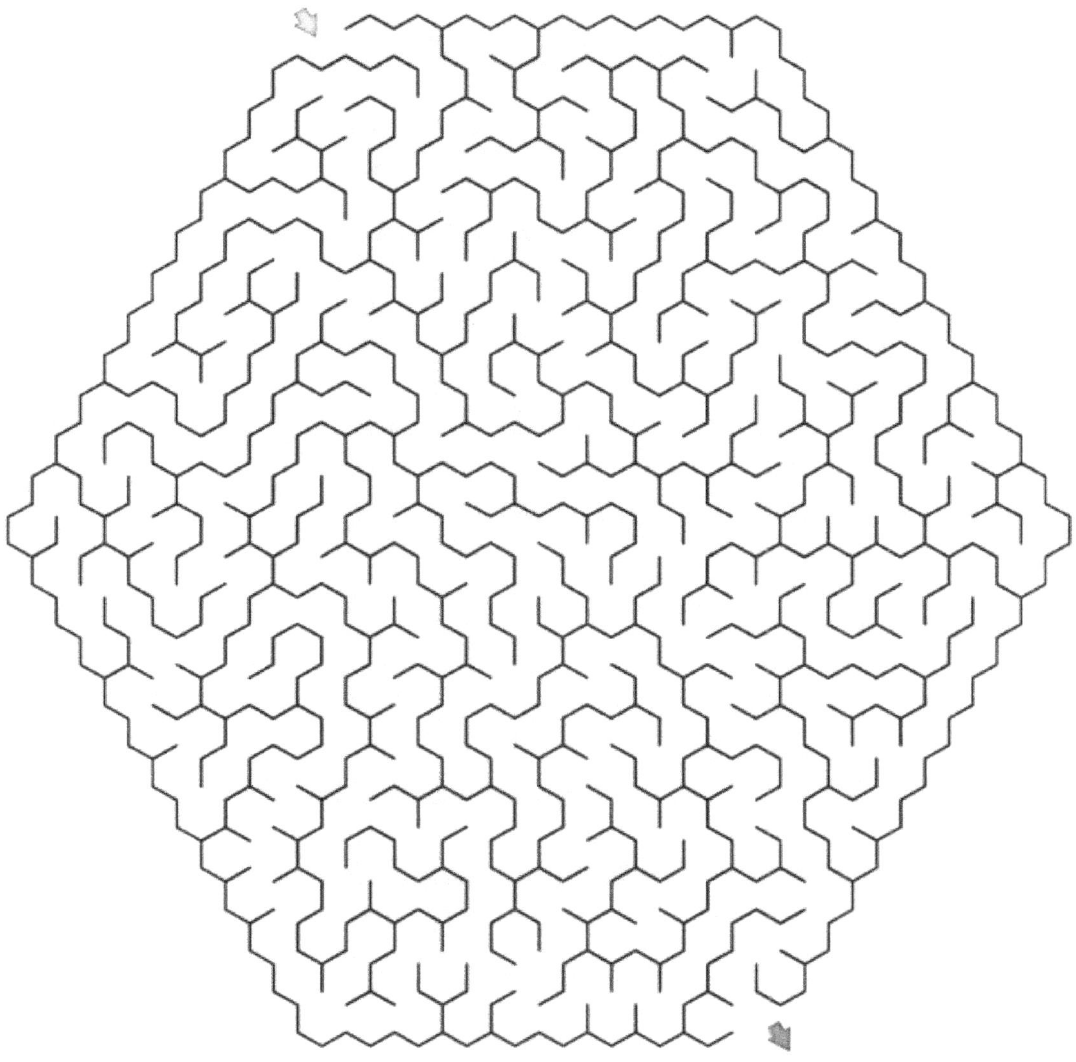

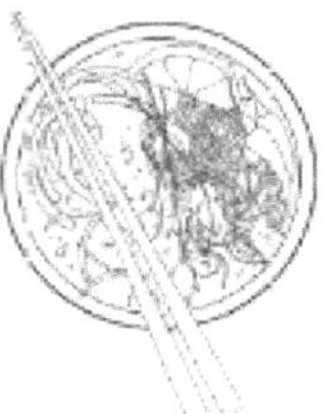

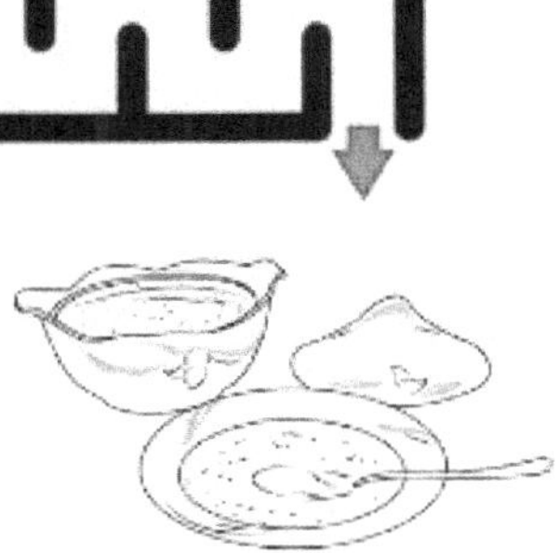